WHEN BEAR STOLE THE CHINOOK

A SIKSIKA TALE

RETOLD AND ILLUSTRATED BY

HARRIET PECK TAYLOR

FARRAR STRAUS GIROUX

NEW YORK

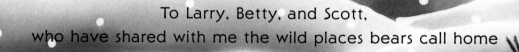

To Larry, Betty, and Scott,
who have shared with me the wild places bears call home

ACKNOWLEDGMENT
The author would like to thank Beverly Reingold and Filomena Tuosto,
editor and designer, for their insight and guidance.

Published simultaneously in Canada by HarperCollins*CanadaLtd*
Color separations by Hong Kong Scanner Arts
Printed in the United States of America by Worzalla. Designed by Filomena Tuosto
First edition, 1997

Library of Congress Cataloging-in-Publication Data
Taylor, Harriet Peck.
    When Bear stole the chinook : a Siksika tale / retold and illustrated by Harriet Peck Taylor. — 1st ed.
      p.   cm.
    Summary: Because the long, hard winter caused scarcity of firewood and food, a poor Indian boy and
his animal friends journey to the lodge of the great Bear to release the chinook.
    ISBN 0-374-10947-8
    1. Siksika Indians—Folklore. 2. Chinook winds—Folklore. [1. Siksika Indians—Folklore. 2. Indians of North
America—Folklore. 3. Folklore—Great Plains.] I. Title.
    E99.S54T39 1997   398.2'089973 — dc20
                                                                                                    96-33843

The north wind blew in hard and cold that long-ago winter. There were many blizzards, and the land was frozen under ice and snow. It seemed that the warm wind called the chinook would never come. The deep snows made it hard to find wood for fires, and there was very little for the Siksika people and the animals to eat.

Each sunrise, the Old Ones would look for signs that the chinook was coming. The chinook would blow in if the skies were clear and blue. But each day was as gloomy as the next, with fog and clouds covering the mountain peaks.

Among the Siksika was a boy with no mother or father. He lived in the poorest of lodges, and his closest companions were the birds and animals. He spoke with them and shared with them whatever food he had.

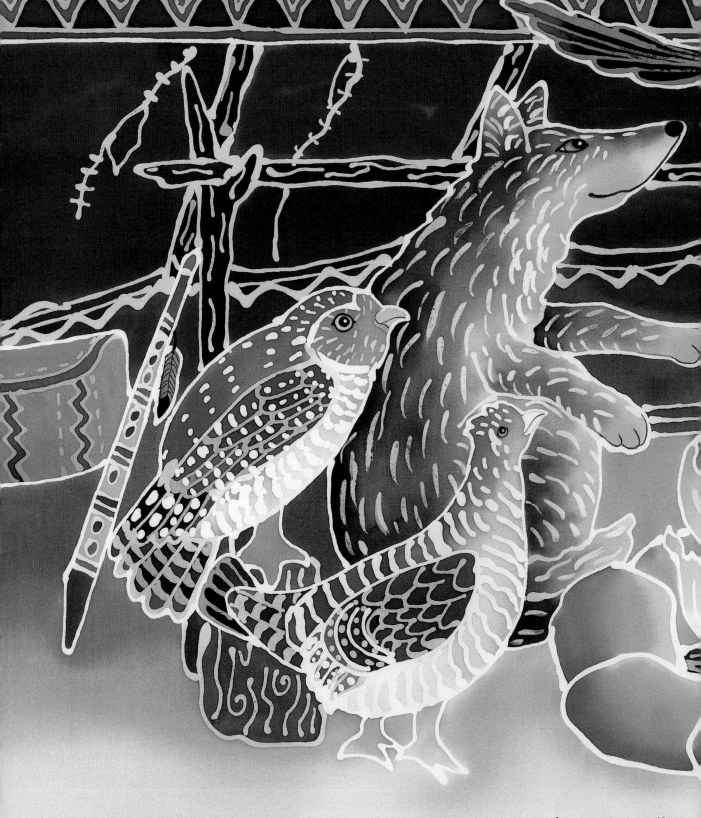

One day he decided to call his friends together for a council. Owl and Coyote came. Weasel, Prairie Chicken, and Magpie were there, too.

The boy turned to Magpie, a busybody who always flew here

and there, learning everyone else's business. "Do you know where the chinook has gone?" he asked.

Magpie answered, "I don't, but my relatives who live in the mountains might know something. I'll go pay them a visit."

The next day he returned and said, "My relatives know a huge Bear who has his den high in the mountains. He has stolen the chinook so that he may keep warm all through the winter."

The friends held another council that evening. They decided to make the long journey to the great Bear's den to try to bring back the chinook.

They left early in the morning, carrying with them dried meat and berries and the boy's stone pipe.

Magpie knew the way and led them up the steep mountain. Higher and higher they climbed, over icy ridges and through snow-covered forests. The wild north wind picked up the snow and threw it in their faces, but still they struggled on. At night they found shelter in caves, huddling together under a buffalo robe for warmth.

At last Magpie announced, "We're near the den of the great Bear. We must go slowly and sneak up on him."

Creeping quietly, they heard a frightening sound. *"Grrrr!"* Bear growled. "Who's there?"

Because of Owl's keen eyesight, the boy sent him to peek through the smoke hole in Bear's den. Owl's job was to see if he could find the chinook.

But Bear was on his guard and heard Owl. When Owl poked his head through the hole, Bear grabbed a stick and knocked him in the eyes. That is why, to this day, owls have circles around their eyes.

"Oow! Oow!" cried Owl as he flew back.

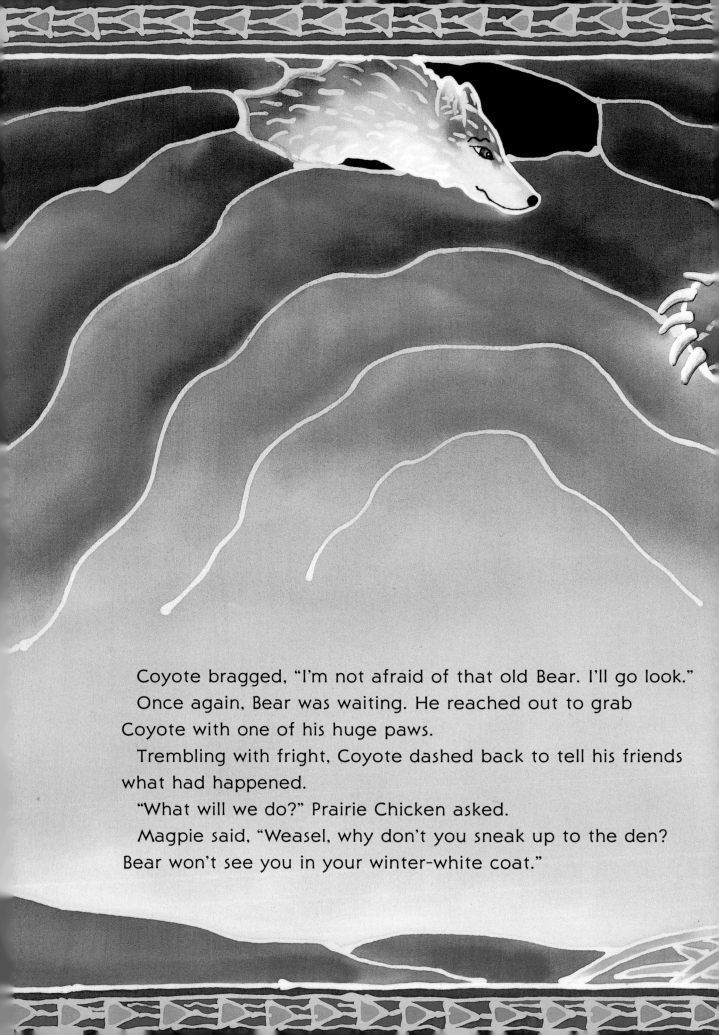

Coyote bragged, "I'm not afraid of that old Bear. I'll go look."

Once again, Bear was waiting. He reached out to grab Coyote with one of his huge paws.

Trembling with fright, Coyote dashed back to tell his friends what had happened.

"What will we do?" Prairie Chicken asked.

Magpie said, "Weasel, why don't you sneak up to the den? Bear won't see you in your winter-white coat."

Weasel crept up to the den. When Bear saw the white fur, he thought snow was falling through his smoke hole, so Weasel was able to get a good look inside.

Weasel returned and whispered, "I have found the chinook. Bear keeps it in a buffalo-hide bag in the far corner of his den. Bear looks huge and fierce! How will we ever get it?"

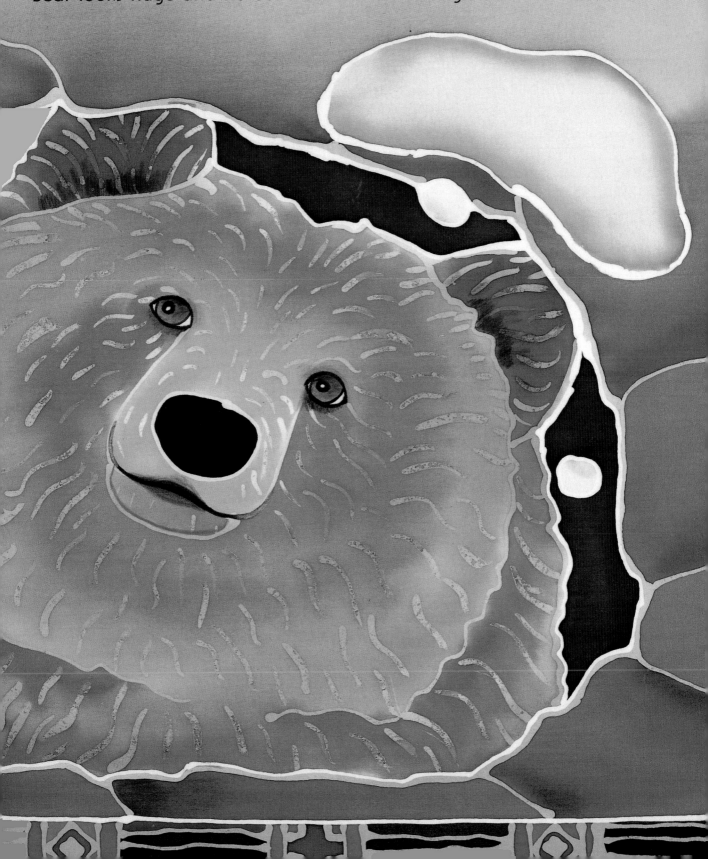

Suddenly the boy had an idea. "I'll blow smoke from my pipe into his den. When it starts to fill with smoke, Bear will become sleepy." The boy got out his pipe and filled it with tobacco. Then he climbed up to the smoke hole and puffed and puffed and puffed. Soon thick white clouds filled the den.

Bear's eyes became heavy and he yawned: *"Aahhh."* Pretty soon, the great Bear's snoring was so loud that even the ground rumbled.

Coyote crawled silently past Bear and grabbed the buffalo-hide bag that held the chinook. Carefully, he dragged it outside, where they saw that it was tied with heavy leather thongs.

Prairie Chicken stepped up and said, "Let me see if I can cut the thongs with my beak." She pecked hard and fast at the leather straps until they snapped and the bag fell open. The chinook rushed out with a loud *whoooosh*!

Bear heard the noise and came thundering out of his den.
The boy and his friends ran like the wind, with Bear's sharp
teeth snapping at their heels. They raced along the icy ridge
and across a frozen river.

When Bear got to the riverbank, the ice was already melting.
He knew it would not hold his weight, so he growled and
paced while Coyote, Magpie, Prairie Chicken, Weasel, Owl,
and the boy escaped safely down the mountain.

When the boy returned to his village, the people came out of their lodges. The boy pointed to the clearing sky. Then the wonderful warm wind blew off the peak and down into the valley, and from there it spread to the far corners of the earth. Everywhere snow and ice melted and the rivers broke up and tumbled down the hillsides. The people, animals, and birds danced and gave thanks under the bright blue sky.

Bear has never again been allowed to steal the chinook. Since he cannot stand the cold, from that time on he has slept all winter long. And that is why bears never leave their dens until the warm wind called the chinook returns, bringing spring to the land.

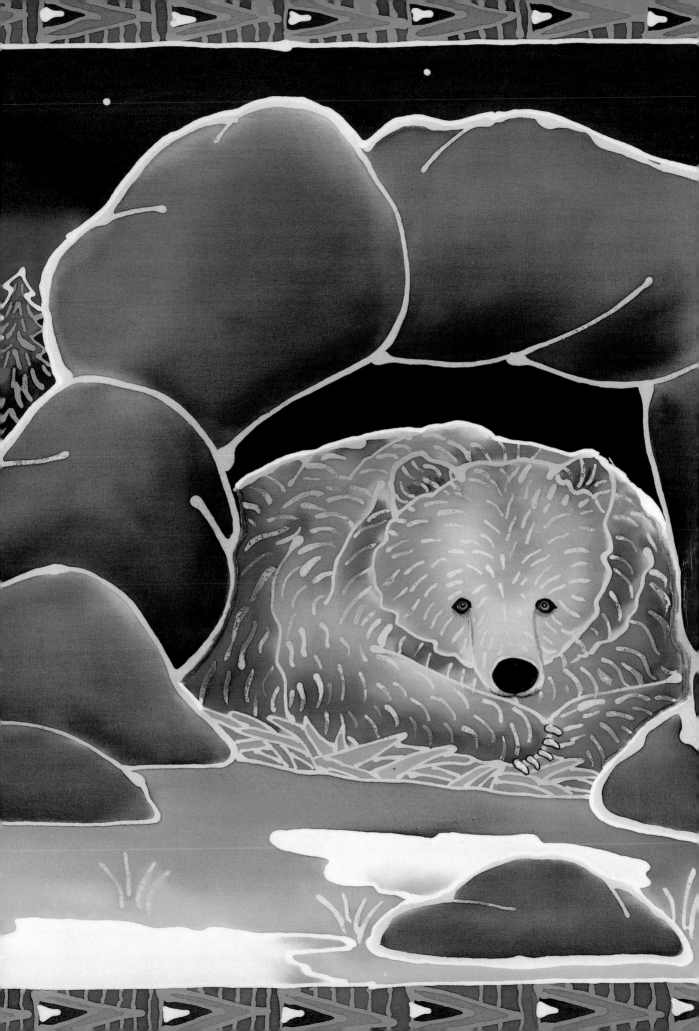

AUTHOR'S NOTE

When Bear Stole the Chinook was adapted from *The Bear Who Stole the Chinook: Tales from the Blackfoot*, by Frances Fraser. Frances Fraser grew up near the Siksika reserve in southern Alberta, Canada. She had friends among the Siksika, then called the Blackfoot, and they asked her to write down their tales because "the time was approaching when the stories would be lost forever."

Siksika means "Black-footed People," and at one time they may have dyed their moccasins black. Long ago, the Siksika lived in the forests farther north. Eventually they drifted southward into what is now southern Alberta, where they occupy the wide plains east of the Rocky Mountains.

Theirs is a cold climate with long winters. That is why the chinook was so important to them. The chinook is the warm, dry wind that blows down from the Rocky Mountains. As it roars eastward onto the plains, it melts snow and seems to bring the breath of spring.

In this story we learn how the Siksika viewed the bear. They both feared the bear for his power and size and admired him for his humanlike qualities. They felt a kinship to the bear. He was a furry person, a relative who went to a den to sleep all winter long. When he emerged at the first signs of spring, it was a time of celebration, marking the end of the long winter.

SOURCES

Fraser, Frances. *The Bear Who Stole the Chinook: Tales from the Blackfoot*. Vancouver: Douglas & McIntyre, 1990.

Grinnell, George Bird. *Blackfoot Lodge Tales: The Story of a Prairie People*. Lincoln, Neb.:
    University of Nebraska Press, 1962.

Linderman, Frank B. *Blackfeet Indians*. St. Paul, Minn.: Great Northern Railway, 1935.

Rockwell, David. *Giving Voice to Bear*. Niwot, Colo.: Roberts Rinehart Publishers, 1991.

Waldman, Carl. *Encyclopedia of Native American Tribes*. New York: Facts on File, 1988.

Wissler, Clark. *A Blackfoot Source Book*. Edited by David Hurst Thomas. New York: Garland Publishing, 1986.